The Overlord Manual

for Babies

volume 1

C. N. Boone

Boonetastic Books

For Hugo and Lily. It is a privilege and honor to be your mother...I mean underling!

Acknowledgments

The author would like to thank her husband, Curt Boone, without whom this book would not have been made. Thank you for encouraging me to imagine, explore, and embark on the next great adventure.

Contents:

The foundational lessons you will need to enjoy your reign as Master of All Things.

Congratulations little Overlord! By commanding your minions to prokure this manual for you, you have taken the first step to becoming a successful Master of All Things. But before you can rule the world, you must first become ruler of your home and everyone in it.

1

Once you learn to rule your house, you'll be well on your way to enjoying a life of absolute power. Now, I'm not sure if you are aware of this, but your ~~parents~~/ underlings will pretty much love you no matter what you do.

in order to make your overlord ship a success you must remeber to always exployt the unwavering love they have for you as much as you possibly can.

3

In this volume I will teach you how to achieve maximum love exployta- tion and thus lay a strong foundation to ensure your reign as overlord is one that will endure. So let's begin.

5

Lesson One: It's never too early to assert yourself as Lord and Master of All Things.

>:{ -Rememeber you may be small, but this does not diminish your all powerfulness.

Many babies who aspire to become overlords make the mistake of pretending to be good babies for a while and in turn are never able to make the transition to becoming an overlord.

It is my suggestion that you set the

tone for your overlordship even

before they leave the hospital with

you. Let them know right away that

you are mighty and not to be tri-

fled with!

8

Helpful tips for letting your underlings know who's boss before getting home.

a.) Eat only when you want to, NOT when they want you to.

>:{ —remeber YOUR the boss! Not them! If you feel like napping or playing during a feeding...GO for it!

Just wail for food whenever you

feel like it. I promise they will always

give it to you.

"Why?", you ask. Because they love

you! They want you to thrive and

grow so they will do everything hu-

manly possible to ensure that you

do.

>:{ -Remeber you are setting the tone.

Ok, moving on...

b.) squirm as much as you can to make diapering more difficult.

This one is simple. It's cold! Let them know you are not pleased by squirming and wailing. They will still have to change you regularly, but it's im-

portant for them to know how you

really feel about it.

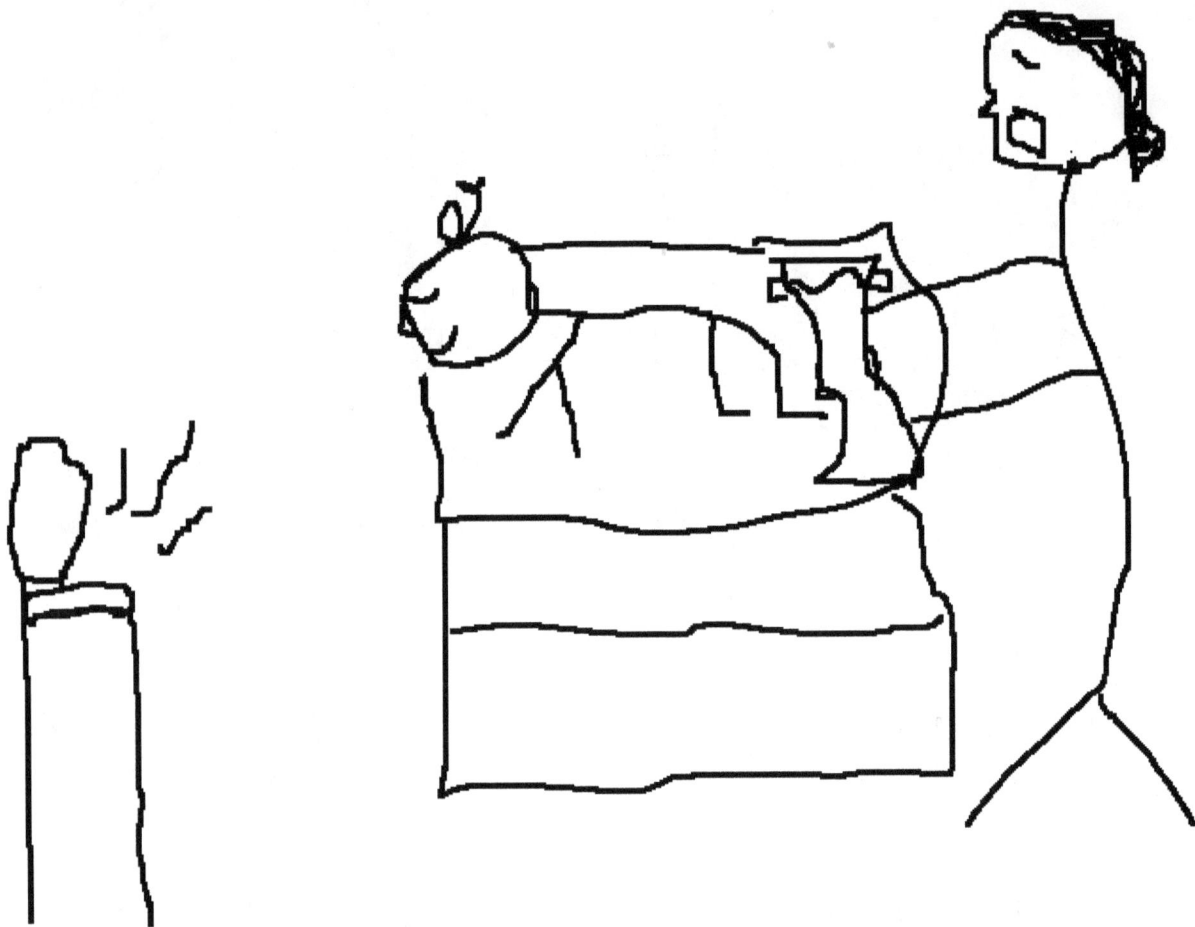

12

c.) when sleeping, lie perfectly still.

They will always think something is wrong and become very nervous. Do this and you will have them on edge by the time they get you home. The more they anxiously hover over you the easier it is to control them.

>:{ -anxious underlings are Obedient

underlings!

Good job so far little overlord! If you have taken my advice the tone of your overlordship has been set and your underlings have started to bend to your will.

You are now ready to move on to the next lesson.

Lesson Two: You must resist the

"schedule" at ALL costs.

As soon as your underlings, get you

home, they will immediately try to

brainwash you and lull you into a

state of passivity by imposing what they

call a "schedule".

16

17

Make no mistake, the schedule has been used for centuries to thwart hundreds of baby overlords all over the world.

The most effective way to destroy the "schedule" is to master the fine art of psychological torture.

"Psychological torture!?", you say.

18

I know it sounds harsh, but trust me

no underling has ever been physically

harmed during the process of mas-

tering lesson two. It's good to

know you are a benevolent over

lord, by being so, your reign should

last well into your teens. At least.

Now, there are about eleven widely known tactics used to accomplish psychological torture, however we will be working to your baby overlord strengths and focus on only three of these.

"Why only three?", you ask. well little

overlord, it will be difficult for your underlings to take your empty threats of bodily harm seriously when you have yet to master the skill of speaking. It will end up sounding like babble and in turn they'll think it's cute.

>:{ -cuteness is a double edged

sword that in this instance will only un-

dermine your ultimate authority

over all things.

That being said the three tactics you

should master are as follows.

Tactic 1. Exposure to unpleasant

sounds for a long period of time.

Tactic 2. sleep depravation.

Tactic 3. shaming and public humiliation.

Let's discuss each one a little more.

Tactic 1 will be one of the most

powerful weapons you have in your

miniature arsenal.

The effects of which can cause hearing loss, anxiety, and Tactic 2 - sleep depravation.

I have one word for you...cry. That's right cry, as loud as you can for as long as you can. If your underlings can never console you, this will work to slowly eat away at their self-esteem and their sanity. The more inadequate they feel the less likely they are to try imposing the schedule on you. It's only logical that with little confidence your underlings will doubt not only the efficacy of trying a schedule, but also their overall effectiveness as a parent in general.

Less confident underlings are far easier to control than the ones who think they know it all.

The beauty of all three tactics is they tie in to one another for easy use. Tactic 1 ties into Tactic

2 because by exposing your underlings

to incessant crying their sleep patterns

will be disrupted and deprivation is

then achieved!

Sleep deprivation will cause confusion,

irritability, and depression. The results

of which will be a state one could

only describe as desperate to

please YOU at all costs. Achieving

sleep depravation and moving your

underlings into the aforementioned

state is best done by either

A) utilizing Tactic 1 at night when they

are most exhausted so that YOU

can rest during the day when they are

forced to stay awake and care for

you, or

B) Falling asleep only when held by an

underling, while in a chair, and utilizing

Tactic 1 if they should ever attempt

to put you down.

Either is effective, but Option B

gives you the ability to inflict physical

discomfort in addition to mental

angst.

30

Okay little Overlord good job

keeping pace! I know this is a lot to

take in, but remember no one ever

said being a successful Overlord

would be easy.

Now that you have mastered Tactics

1 and 2 it's time to bring everything

together with the third and final tactic you will use use to master the fine art of psychologically torturing your underlings into submission to your ultimate authority.

Let's review. By the time you begin to make use of Tactic 3 your underlings are anxious, confused, depressed and desperate to please you at all costs. They should also be very insecure. It's important for you to understand that in general underlings are proud and very sensitive to the opinions of other underlings. It's important for you to do all can to ensure they continue to

33

feel that they are not doing a

good job.

"How do I accomplish that?", you ask.

Patience tiny dictator I will explain. It's

important for the first year to re

serve any smiles, indulgence in maniacal

laughter, and general overlord mile

stones exclusively for your underlings

34

In the privacy of your new domain. By doing so when your underlings tell other underlings of things you've accomplished yet will show no evidence of, they will slowly start to lose credibility with their peers ensuring their low self-esteem will continue to keep them passive.

36

If you utilize Tactic 1 every time they take you out in public little by little they will come to believe they really are poor at parenting and the accompanying sense of shame and embarrassment will ensure you smooth sailing through what will be only the beginning of your terrible reign!

so little overlord, you should feel

proud of yourself!

38

You successfully completed and hopefully have begun to master the first two lessons in baby overlordship.

If at anytime you feel that your mighty overlordness is waning or that your underlings might rebel against you, please refer back to this manual as needed.

One last thing...If your underlings should ever catch you in the act of making evul plans, be sure to eat them, and then spit them up later.

www.ingramcontent.com/pod-product-compliance
Lightning Source LLC
Chambersburg PA
CBHW081547040426
42448CB00015B/3250